MW00712163

My Cup Runneth Over:
Overcoming the Spirit of Rejection

By: Dr. Tandria M. Callins

HeartInk Press LLC

Take note that Jesus, Christ, Lord and God are referred to as He, as well as, he in this book. This purpose is to make sure no one gets confused with ownership and point of subject in particular areas of the book.

Heart.Ink Press, LLC
P.O. Box 6312
Tallahassee, FL 32314

"Manifesting Dreams and Visions…
…Tuned to the Beat of Your Heart"

ISBN: 978-0-9835854-0-4

Content

Chapters

Acknowledgments

When I think back through the experiences of my life, I realize they are the experiences that make up the clay that has shaped my life today. Without those important ingredients or experiences, you would not be reading this book today.

I would like to thank my Heavenly Father for "ordaining me from my mother's womb." From my mother's womb, the enemy already had a plan for my demise. I was born with an infection that nearly cost me my life. As a teenager, a gun was put to my head, and once again my life was threatened. God, through His grace and mercy, has allowed me to live to share my testimony and to lead many to deliverance. God, I know it's not about me, but it is all about You. I love you.

To my husband, my Pastor, my friend, and my lover, Calvin "Pee Wee" Callins, Sr., I thank you for your unconditional love and support. You have been my coach and cheerleader throughout our entire lives together and I am forever indebted to you. I am, because you are sacrificing, kind, warm, sensitive, encouraging, thoughtful, and unselfish. I love you. Always. Forever. Still. For real though.

To my children Calaydria, Calvin Jr., and Caleb, thank you for allowing mommy time to write. It is because of the three of you that I am so passionate about what I'm writing. You all will lead the next generation to deliverance. I pray that through my transparency and desire to heal women and men of their childhood ghosts, that you all will do the same in your own way. I love you.

To my mom, Fresh Celeste, and sister, Tisha, I'm writing this for us. We will be connected forever through our experiences. I thank God for his protection over our lives. I thank God for how he kept our minds. We are survivors! Thank you both for believing in me and supporting me with ALL of my accomplishments. You all have been in the background for many years assisting me in every transition of my life. I love you.

To my dad, although estranged, I thank you. It's because of you I have something to write about. I love you.

To Greater New Hope Anointed Ministries, thank you for your support and prayers. I also extend a special thanks to the armor bearers and adjutants. Oh, and I can't forget my personal hair, wardrobe, and image consultants. I love you.

To Heart Ink Press, thank you for allowing me this opportunity to share my testimony through written form. Thank you for embellishing my thoughts and ideas and turning this project into a creative work of art. I love you.

Preface

"My Cup Runneth Over"- Overcoming the Spirit of Rejection

"My Cup Runneth Over" comes from the heart of broken women who have decided by either choice or force to bottle up their deep and most intimate personal challenges. We've been portrayed through the years as "strong black women" who are recognized as having the innate ability to endure hardship and pain. From my experiences, this portrayal has handicapped us from being transparent and true testimonies of God's healing and delivering power.

We have hid behind the facade of a "strong black woman" so long that we have become paralyzed to truth and have become experts at deception. We have encountered excessive, innumerable, and unimaginable attacks in life that we have become immune to righteous and peaceful living. This is evident throughout our churches by the way we expect failure and instigate strife between one another.

"My Cup Runneth Over" deals with the absence of emptying out before God. Instead of dealing with the root of sin, we pacify the problem and continue on as if there is nothing wrong. When the next problem comes along we push it aside, we never pray about it, we never take it to God, and we continue on with life as usual. Here's the problem. Your cup, "spiritual temple", gets full of unresolved issues and spills over into your natural life and you become a bitter, ungrateful, angry, vengeful, envious woman who's living a miserable life. Your cup runs over into your home, and onto your children, your marriage, your job, and INTO THE CHURCH.

"My Cup Runneth Over" deals with one major by-product, the Spirit of Rejection. I begin the conversation with two roots of this Spirit, which is childhood molestation and broken father-daughter relationships.

This book is designed to minister to you in areas that are considered taboo in the church. I want to help you to reflect and commune with the Holy Spirit regarding your deep hurts, wounded spirits, unspoken requests, and the unforgiveness that rest in your heart.

I encourage you to utilize the "Dear Jesus" letters to express to God your inner most feelings. Let healing begin. Let deliverance begin. Let reconciliation begin. Don't let your cup run over with defeat, regret, guilt, bitterness, anger, deception, envy, rebellion, or strife. But fill your cup with joy, peace, love, forgiveness, freedom, and laughter.

Introduction

A visiting Evangelist at church was closing out her sermon and reflecting on her work with a shelter for battered and abused women. She began giving her testimony about being molested and overcoming the emotional and spiritual struggles she had faced. As she was speaking, the Lord began speaking to my spirit.

Vividly, I remember feeling a burning sensation all over my body. My heart started pounding as if someone was knocking on my heart's door. The Lord was instructing me to openly confess my experiences of being molested. He whispered, "It's not for you but it's for someone else to get healed and delivered. Someone is trapped inside and wants to be released from bondage." God pressed in my spirit that he wanted to use me as a vessel.

Not knowing the consequences of confessing being a victim of sexual abuse, I frantically peered in and out of the pews to see who was there. Can I trust strangers with this soul shattering secret? What is my husband going to say? I never uttered a word to my mother, what is she going to say? It was as if I was experiencing an out-of-body moment. My feet began walking towards the pulpit. I reached for the microphone. My husband rested his hand upon my shoulder as if he knew what I was about to do. I no longer controlled my own body. My mouth opened and it seemed as if I was talking in slow motion. The words that I sheltered, protected, and threw the key away from, escaped freely. All I could hear were the beats of my heart pounding louder and louder. I thought, "I'm the FIRST LADY, they can't know what I've been through. I have my family in here. What are they going to say? Who are they going to suspect? Will I have to press charges?" THUMP! ....THUMP! ....THUMP! ....THUMP!

After my confession, silence killed the air. Oh, my God, what have I just done? I can't believe I just put myself out there like that. How will my husband and I recover from this? I couldn't stand the silence. What's next?

And then to my surprise, a guest Pastor stood up from the pulpit, "I too have been molested." Then like popcorn, all over the sanctuary, from the pulpit to the back door, one-by-one, women popped up from their seats...I was molested, I was sexually abused. Screams, screeching, and outbursts began to ring out from each corner of the sanctuary as we began to expose the devil. Years and years of abuse, secrecy, built up frustration, shame, guilt, hurt, resentment, anger, hatred was let out in the atmosphere.

It was then I realized what God wanted to do through me. He opened the door for deliverance to take place; and deliverance is only capable through transparency. Jeremiah 30:12 "your wounds are incurable, your injury beyond healing, but I will restore your health and heal your wounds." John 5:6, Jesus asked the man if he wanted to be healed. Confess that you want to be healed.

We have to go through the painful process of transformation; the excruciating elimination of parts of ourselves in order to become who we were created to be. We have to be willing to have our wounds exposed and cleansed. James 5:16 reads, "Confess your faults, one to another, and pray for one another, that ye may be healed. The effectual, fervent prayer of a righteous man, availeth much."

It's time to break this generational curse of childhood molestation. Begin the conversations with your children. Heal yourself with confession. It's good for the soul.

Dear Jesus,

_____

_____

_____

_____

_____

_____

_____

_____

_____

_____

_____

_____

_____

_____

_____

_____

_____

_____

_____

_____

_____

_____

_____

_____

_____

_____

_____

_____

Sincerely,

Me

Chapter 1

Daddy's Little Girl

Have you ever wondered why a baby's first word is "dada?" Whether the father is around or not, the toddler usually finds a way to babble those infamous words "dada." As much as we hate to admit it mothers, you know what I'm talking about. We'll engage in playful banter with our child just to repeat the words "mama." And it seems that the harder we try, the louder they get, "dada."

A daughter's relationship with her father is the first male-female relationship she experiences. It is from dad that she gains her first reflection of herself as a female, she develops a sense of acceptance or non-acceptance, she learns to be valued or discounted, and her self-concept is shaped. During this developing father-daughter relationship, she regards herself as she thinks others regard her. In other words, if she is esteemed as "daddy's little girl," or his "little princess," or his "little angel," then that is the persona she will uphold.

Starting at an early age, in search of honest opinions that really count, daughters are eager to communicate with their fathers. Eventually, ongoing and reciprocal communication between a father and daughter develops a daughter's assuredness and assertiveness and is transcended into her lifestyle. However, if dad rejects me or criticizes me, I'm not good enough (Perkins, 2001).

The first love of every daughter is their father. When the father is around and gives love and attention, his daughter(s) grow up full of love and compassion. The girl usually doesn't lack love or feel emptiness because she received it first from the first guy who tells her that he loves her. On the other hand, girls without fathers search for security and love that they never received from their own fathers. As a result, she forgoes all inhibitions and succumbs to the advances of the first male figure in her life who deceptively utters the most powerful words, "I love you." Surprisingly, without resistance, the girl becomes susceptible to a cycle of emotional, mental, and physical abuse only to fulfill her hunger and thirst for love and attention.

The repeated cycles of rejection from my father led me in a downward spiral. Looking for love and security from an older man became inevitable. The overwhelming feelings of emptiness and loneliness steered me into the arms of boys and men that cared nothing for me. Rejection from my first love, my father, the absence of his affection and attention clouded my judgment from right and wrong. As a pre-teen, I didn't exactly know what I was missing. I believe the enemy had a trap for me at an early age. Since there was no spiritual covering in the house, my sister and I were vulnerable to the enemy's devices. God knew what and who I was destined to be and the devil was trying to deter me from my destiny. According to Romans 8:28-31,

"And we know that in all things God works for the good of those who love him, who have been called according to his purpose. For those God foreknew he also predestined to be conformed to the likeness of his Son, that he might be the firstborn among many brothers. And those he predestined, he also called; those he called, he also justified; those he justified, he also glorified. What, then, shall we say in response to this? If God is for us, who can be against us?"

What is so mind boggling is that after repeated cycles of rejection, I never stopped wanting to be with dad, I never stopped wanting his approval, and I never stopped wanting to be his little girl. It's like being in an abusive relationship but not being able to let go or not having the courage to leave or get out. We had spurts of fun and good times. I guess that's what fueled my desire to keep working at our relationship. I wanted to show him that I turned out to be a good girl and that I was someone he could be proud of.

According to research, women experience pain when she feels abandoned by her father because she is no longer his little princess, or admiring disciple, or his little angel (Freud, 1988). Secunda (1992) described a woman's father as her "first love," regardless of her experience with her father. Father-daughter relationships have the potential to shape interaction patterns that surface as women enter into adult relationships. The psychological premise most commonly cited in research is that women with abusive or absent fathers have difficulty with men and often choose husbands who abuse or abandon them.

Well-fathered daughters are usually more self confident, more self-reliant, and more successful in school and in their careers than poorly fathered daughters (Perkins, 2001). Daughters with loving, comfortable, communicative relationships with their fathers are also less likely to develop eating disorders. In short, a father's impact on his daughter's life is far reaching and lifelong (Neilson, 2006).

According to Joe Kelly (2003), the primary male role model in a girl's life is her father. Fathers influence their daughters in profound ways from how they see themselves to what they come to expect from men and the world at large. Childhood relationships you had with the parent of the opposite sex has had the most influence on the adult you have become. How you feel about yourself as a woman goes back to how your Daddy treated his little girl, you (Kelly, 2003).

By looking at the relationships that you've had with other men you can tell whether or not you gravitate to men like your father? Are they usually kind and loving men or uncaring and abusive? Daughters need to know that the first man in their life loved them unconditionally as every man in her life thereafter will be patterned after her first love—good, bad, or indifferent (Kelly, 2003).

If you were fortunate to have a father who enriched your life and made you feel like his beautiful princess, intelligent, and an independent individual then your relationships with men in your life will yield positive experiences. On the other hand, if you lived with a father who discounted you and made you feel miserable or if you had an absentee father who was not a part of your life then it is likely you will be attracted to that same type of man. One would think that after living with an alcoholic, abusive, or inattentive, emotionally unavailable father would make you more aware and thus more cautious and selective. Unfortunately, the opposite of the established pattern is more prevalent (Kelly, 2003).

The psychology behind this phenomenon is that being treated in an abusive way as a child diminishes your self-worth and thus your expectations of yourself and the way others should treat you. You forget that you deserve choices in your life and tend to accept whatever circumstances befall you. Moreover, most abusive, aggressive men prefer women they can easily dominate;

your diminished self-image makes you a target for abuse. A vicious cycle of reduced self-worth and abusive relationships ensue because treatment only enforces the poor self-esteem. Breaking the pattern is essential if you are ever to enjoy a healthy relationship with the opposite sex (Kelly, 2003).

Fathers are the first to impact girls in the following areas:

- Self-respect: A daughter often learns self-respect and respect of men in the relationship with her dad. It is an excellent training ground for girls to learn self-pride and respect for others. If the father is fair and listens to his daughter's thoughts, she will gain self confidence and assurance that her beliefs are correct.

- Assertiveness: When daughters have a solid communication pattern with their dads and feel heard, they develop assertiveness with others.

Combativeness in women often comes from a belief that they are powerless. They learn to exercise strength without unkindness through their dads.

- Affection: Girls develop clear ideas about what is right or wrong in physical touching. They learn that they can be safe with certain males and that they are regarded as people with boundaries. They will set appropriate boundaries with other males.

- Expectations of Men: Based on how her father acted, a daughter will often determine what their expectations are of men. A father who is protective of his daughter's interests, physical and emotional, will help her believe that she is worth honoring.

Are you a son or daughter who is suffering from a broken relationship with your earthly father? Are you still stuck in the "if I had...or if he'd been around...or I wish I would have had...?"

Dear Jesus,

_____

_____

_____

_____

_____

_____

_____

_____

_____

_____

Sincerely,

_Me_

Chapter 2

The Spirit of Rejection

Rejection is a big issue that many face in the church today. Because of our fear of rejection, we live our lives as a slave to what people think of us, instead of living up to what God thinks of us. If we continue to live only up to what people think, we'll never please everyone. All that matters is that we please God. In Galatians 1:10, we are reminded that, "If pleasing people were my goal, I would not be Christ's servant" (Parks, 2006).

To reject means "to throw away," "discard." Rejection is the act of "being denied love." The feeling of being discarded leads us to believe that we are unloved. When we feel unloved, we deem ourselves worthless. As much as we feel rejected, unloved, and worthless that is how much we are unable to receive love, whether from God or people. Often, we hear when people tell us they love us, but we don't truly recognize that love for the gift that it is. Instead, we wait for the proverbial "other shoe" to drop, and anxiously anticipate when that love will be withdrawn (Parks, 2006).

The enemy, Satan, is a liar, a thief and a murderer. He's a liar because he tries to convince us that what he is saying (through our perceptions) is true – that we are worthless, unloved, and uncared for. This idea directly contradicts Scripture. In many passages, we are told of our value in God's sight. He is a thief, because he tries to steal our faith, our peace, our joy, and our freedom in Christ. In fact, in the Greek, the word for "steal" is "klepto". Just as in life, too often, theft isn't noticed until it's too late. He is a murderer because he wants us to give ourselves over to worthless pursuits – things that are empty and void of any purpose or plan, thereby "killing" any chance we have to engage in meaningful, Kingdom-building activity. He is a destroyer because he destroys (completely ruins) lives and causes regret over things undone or dreams not pursued (Parks, 2006).

But, the grace that shines through is this: Jesus is the opposite of all of that – the antidote, the remedy! He's Truth personified. He restores instead of stealing. He rebuilds instead of tearing down, and that which He rebuilds is beautiful. He is Life itself! In laying down His life, He restores life to us (Parks, 2006).

The Enemy is tricky – he knows that he can only really make us ineffective by hitting us where it's most vital – our faith and love. He makes us self-centered so that we cannot function in the full assurance and power of our faith. He takes the joy and peace we once knew and replaces it, over time little-by-little, with rejection, fear, and pain (Parks, 2006).

In Chapter 3 of "Ministering Freedom to The Emotionally Wounded," the author addresses "Overcoming

Rejection." This chapter refers to the four "walls" of rejection (Parks, 2006).

The four "walls" of rejection are:

Rejection of God: God says in His word that we are His children and that we are made in His image – beautiful. Anytime we think less of ourselves than this, we are, in effect, rejecting His word, and by connection, Him.

Fear of Rejection: We want everyone to like us. But, at the same time, we tend to sabotage our relationships. We don't keep in touch like we should. We get close to someone and then pull back. Could it be that we are afraid of losing them at some point? Is it that, maybe, by being in control of when the relationship ends, we won't feel rejected because we are doing the rejecting? It's a vicious cycle – we try to run from relationships because we don't want to risk being hurt – but in doing so, we feel more rejection, and so the next time we have the chance to enter a relationship, we withdraw further, adding more perceived rejection. It's hard to trust people when we are caught up in a cycle of rejection – always wondering when they will end up not liking us for whatever reason. So often, it feels like it is easier to not even get involved.

Self-Rejection: Have you ever watched Sesame Street when they had the "One of these things just doesn't belong here, one of these things just isn't the same" segments – a group of things where three are similar, but one is actually different? When dealing with rejection, we can feel like the one thing that wasn't the same – out of place. But, to think that the first sacrifice ever (Genesis 3:21) was made so that Adam and Eve could have a permanent covering for their "shame" reminds us that Jesus' sacrifice covers us from our hopelessness, worthlessness and worse.

Rejection of Others: A lot of people have hurt us over the years – some intentionally, some not. It's hard to let go of that hurt. We have to remember that forgiveness is a choice, not a feeling. We may not feel like hugging the people that hurt us, but we can still choose to forgive them. In forgiving, we release our pain, leaving it at the feet of our Father. Once we release the pain, we ask God to come and fill the hollow places that are left and we ask Him to bless those who have hurt or offended us. We do this so that we can stand before our Father and receive the forgiveness He offers to us (Matthew 6:14-15). We may not feel like we have forgiven, but in that moment, we receive our freedom in Christ from the bitterness that once bound us.

The roots of rejection can be traced back to the womb. From the womb some are under Rejection. There is also Rejection from the Father and Rejection from the Mother. Rejection from the Womb *enters the fetus before birth*. Conceived in lust, and the Bastard curse, *enters* at *the moment* of *conception out* of *wedlock*. With them comes the Curse of Bastard and Lust (I Timothy. 2:8-15; 2 Peter

3:7). "As for my people, children are their oppressors, and women rule over them. Oh, my people, they which lead thee cause thee to err, and destroy the way of thy paths" (Isaiah 3:12).

In Jeremiah 30:17, the Lord promises restoration, health, and healing of the womb. The wounds which come with rejection are deep hurt and wounded spirits, grief, pain, and sorrow (Matthew 8: 16-17; Isaiah. 53:4. Psalm 23). When a person has been rejected from the womb, spirits of lust, whoredom and sensuality will enter. Rejection from the womb opens the door to harlotry. Rebellion works rejection. With rebellion also come hatred, anger, bitterness and others. You can cast out other demons, but you MUST seek the root of the problem, and often this is rejection. Ask the Lord to send fierce warrior angels to force out all door keepers and root spirits (Moody, 2010). Have them chop out those roots and pull them out, along with the door keepers, to make a clean sweep (Hebrews 4: 15; 7:25; 4: 16). Both deliverance and restoration of the soul are available to the believer (Psalms 147:2-3).

The curse of destruction of the family priesthood (which is centered in the father and is usually the result of inherited family curses) paves the way for the Spirit of Rejection in a child. The father is the priest and head of the home! Frustrated by his lack of leadership and her inability to respect him as a man, the woman (who herself may have inherited curses of dominance) begins to take over and direct the home by the Jezebel spirit. Men go after wine, women, and song - such as adult toys, outdoors, sports, et cetera to escape the wife! The child is caught up in the conflict between the parents and becomes its chief victim. Children are the main victims of divorce! The spirits in the mother will coerce the male child, forbidding him to assert his masculinity or to engage in activities which would develop him as a man. This pattern develops homosexual men (Moody, 2010)!

The progression of destruction in the life of a female child is much the same as that of the boy, except that she will consciously or unconsciously absorb and manifest the same attitudes and spirits which drive her mother. Watch how your children have your same bad habits (Moody, 2010)!

Many people have come to full age still carrying the scars of emotional, physical, or sexual abuse. These men and women look normal but inside they are filled with terrible insecurity, anger, or fear. Others are sitting on a ticking emotional time-bomb of resentment and rebellion, just waiting to boil over into rage. These scars, if left unhealed, will render a person incapable of entering into committed, wholesome, long-term relationships (Wood, 2008).

One particular problem is very common. It undermines the confidence of many Christians and interferes with true fellowship between friends. It is a lying spirit from our enemy called Spirit of Rejection. Rejection is the worst pain the human spirit can suffer. Anyone who has been abandoned, suffered abuse, or endured discrimination can relate to this kind of anguish. Let's examine this assault from Satan so we can recognize this form of mental oppression (Wood, 2008).

First, the Spirit of Rejection refers to the mind-set ingrained into us that tells us that we are unloved, unwanted, or will never be good enough. This may start in childhood. This mind-set makes us strive to earn our acceptance. It makes people feel driven to perform in order to be approved. This mind-set makes people feel they are loved for what they do rather than for who they are. It is demeaning. It robs people of peace. The sad thing is that no amount of achievement is ever enough to satisfy it (Wood, 2008).

In other people, the injustice of being treated unfairly or rejected or disrespected makes them boil over in anger. They quit trying to fit in, rebel against everyone, and try to break out of the box being forced on them. In refusing to be a victim, they may victimize others. Resentment covers their soul like a dark shroud. They wind up in an emotional prison of their own making (Wood, 2008).

The mind-set of rejection is the result of having believed a lie. It is a syndrome of self-talk that comes from being programmed with falsehoods. Having been told a lie often enough, victims begin to say, "Yes, it's true." The lie becomes accepted when the victim agrees with the accusations. They become their own accuser. They have internalized the venom. The deceit becomes a self-fulfilling prophecy. The victim begins to expect to be rejected and thus sabotages his or her own relationships (Wood, 2008).

This mental stronghold of rejection is powerful. It will be torn down only when we find God's Word about our case and choose to believe the truth instead of a lie. Only God's truth can set us free. The truth will connect us to God's love. God's love will cure our wounded souls (Wood, 2008).

Take a moment to think how the enemy has attempted to
destroy the way of your path using the Spirit of Rejection.
Were you given up for adoption? Raised by family
members? Did your parents want to abort you? Were you
called a "mistake" or a "slip-up?" Have you loved
someone, only to be rejected by them?

Dear Jesus,

_____

_____

_____

_____

_____

_____

_____

_____

_____

_____

_____

_____

_____

_____

_____

_____

_____

_____

_____

_____

_____

_____

_____

Sincerely,

Me

Chapter 3

Identity Crisis

When someone is betrayed they may say, "I'll never open myself up again. No one will ever get another chance to hurt me like that again." This is a natural reaction, but dangerous. It will open the door to defensiveness, which is the reaction of somebody that has been hurt once too often. When you have opened yourself and given your all, only to be rejected brings shame and humiliation. Shame is debilitating, and it keeps a person from functioning as a healthy human being (Isaiah 54:4-6).

The most common cause of a "wounded spirit" or a broken heart (as it is commonly called) is rejection. The word rejection can be defined as the experience of being cast off, pushed away, refused or unwanted by another person. In Psalm 55 we can observe that King David experienced some hurt and rejection from someone close to him (L, 2003-2008).

> *For it is not an enemy who reproaches*
> *me, then I could bear it. Nor is it one*
> *who hates me who has exalted himself*
> *against me, then I could hide myself*
> *from him. But it is you, a man my*
> *equal, my companion and my familiar*
> *friend. We who had sweet fellowship*
> *together, walked in the house of God*
> *in the throng.* (Psalm 55: 12-14)

Often we experience hurt from those closest to us such as family or friends. Satan takes advantage of those painful experiences by magnifying them to your heart and mind, pressuring you to believe that those situations are a reflection of your identity and your worth (L, 2003-2008).

Jesus called Satan a *"liar"* and the *"father of lies"* in John 8:44. One strategy that this lying spirit uses against people is to whisper the lie of rejection to the mind and heart. The devil knows the pain and the bondage that a Spirit of Rejection can bring into a person's life if his lie is accepted as truth. The lie of rejection says: "You are a 'reject' and the evidence to prove it can be found in your memories of painful treatment by others" (L, 2003-2008, pg. 3). But the sinful actions of others toward you does not prove you are a "reject," it just proves that people are sinners (L, 2003-2008).

God's Word tells you the truth: you are not rejected and you are not a "reject" even if a multitude of circumstances in your life seem to shout that it is true! The real truth about each of us is found in God's Word: *He made us accepted in the Beloved*...(Ephesians 1:6). God lovingly created you and designed you for a specific purpose in life. You are perfectly accepted and desired by God even if the human beings you have encountered have not treated you that way (L, 2003-2008).

Have you allowed a "Spirit of Rejection" to influence your life unknowingly? Here are some signs:

- You have an expectation that people will overlook you, not appreciate you, or use you.

- You feel bad when other people are praised, honored, promoted, or noticed. You can't rejoice for them because it reminds you of how overlooked, unappreciated, or undervalued you are.

- If you walk into a room and people are talking and they stop when you enter, you immediately assume they were speaking negatively about you.

- You think the worst if your phone calls, e-mails, or messages are not returned immediately. You never think the person might be busy or hasn't gotten the message, you always conclude they are purposely ignoring or avoiding you.

- If someone declines an invitation you have given them, you never believe that their reason is legitimate; you instead attribute rejection of you, as a person, to be their motive.

- You constantly feel slighted by the smallest things including someone not making eye contact with you, failing to greet you in a public setting, or not being invited into a group of people who are chatting.

- You find yourself struggling to be "perfect" because you believe if you are "perfect" you won't be rejected.

- You are strongly motivated to strive to be a high achiever to prove your worth and to obtain recognition and validation from others.

- You find yourself often bragging about your achievements, "showing off", or exaggerating to impress people.

- You are driven to play the role of "savior" or "hero" in order to feel wanted or needed.

- You are critical or demeaning toward others because it makes you feel superior.

- You shy away from making any deep relationships or revealing yourself to others to avoid the anticipated pain of rejection.

- You are unable to trust people or God.

- You are constantly besieged with hopelessness.

- You have an agreement with death. You think others would be better off if you died, or you think no one would notice or miss you if you died, you pray to die, or think that death would be an escape from your pain.

The Spirit of Rejection also refers to the residue within our personality of being deeply wounded. This mental or emotional scarring can occur due to being neglected, abandoned, or abused. It can also come from being betrayed, being shamed, or being made to feel unloved. Racial discrimination often leaves scars of rejection. Children who were abused sexually suffer cruelly from this inner hurt. Divorce can also leave a lingering, festering wound. The fear of being rejected can make a person run from relationships. They reject others before they themselves are rejected. They spiritually "stiff-arm" those who try to get close (Wood, 2008).

Just like you can be injured in your flesh and form a bruise or a scar, so you can be injured in your inner man and develop a sensitive place or perhaps a hardened area like a scab on your feelings. When that irritated place gets touched, a reaction occurs. The Bible speaks of having a "wounded spirit." One symptom of having a wounded spirit is that you feel absolutely nothing, as if you are dead inside. Another symptom is that you are hypersensitive in that area and can explode at the slightest provocation. God's unconditional love, realized and received, can cure this wound (Wood, 2008).

Why do rejection wounds hurt us so deeply?

Rejection wounds hurt us so deeply because it attacks the very person that we are. It destroys our self-esteem, and attacks who we are, and our purpose in life. This is why it is one of the most common tools the devil will use to destroy a person's life. God never wanted us to feel rejected or abandoned. He desires for you to know who you really are, and realize how deeply God loves, accepts, and appreciates you, so that you can live out the fullness of what all God has ordained you to be (Langeland, 2004). God's Word tells us that without being rooted and grounded in the love (and acceptance) of God, we cannot experience the fullness of God in our lives (Ephesians 3:19).

Rejection has a way of destroying a person's life in a way that few other things can. The sad fact is that the number of people who are affected by rejection is staggering. If we want to be all that God has created us to be, then overcoming rejection and it's affects is vital and absolutely essential (Langeland, 2004).

Many people who have faced rejection and abuse as a child grow up with unresolved emotional wounds. Rejection causes emotional wounds, which if not cleansed and released, will grow and fester into spiritual wounds (such as unforgiveness, envy, blaming God, jealousy, et cetera). Those spiritual wounds open us up to evil spirits which love to take advantage of this opportunity to invade us. The goal of the enemy is to get us built up with emotional baggage inside and negative feelings in our hearts against one another, ourselves, and God (Langeland, 2004).

A person who has a hard time admitting they are wrong, or receiving constructive criticism, has an underlying problem with rejection. How do we know that? Because they are basing their identity, who they are, upon their ability to be right about everything. For this same reason, stubbornness can also be rooted in rejection. They have to be right, or else they feel worthless... that's because "who they are" (their identity) is based upon them being right. This also ties in with opinionated personalities, who are always there to tell you all about something, even if they have little or no real understanding to speak from (L, 2003-2008).

Then we have performance orientation and drivenness, certain variances of obsessive compulsive disorders where a person is basing their identity and who they are upon how well they perform at something in life. Whenever we base who we are upon our performance, or our being correct about something, then we fail, it is a blow to our identity (L, 2003-2008).

Those who struggle with rejection can also become what we call fixers; a fixer is a person who is eager to tell everybody else how they need to be doing things, but many times have little understanding or experience in such matters. Such a person attempts to be the Holy Spirit in other people's lives, where they have no authority or right to step in. They find their identity in fixing other people's problems, and they love it when people come to them for help or advice (L, 2003-2008).

The truth is that we were created to be loved, accepted, and appreciated. Rejection is an anti-Christ spirit because it opposes the very nature that God created in us. Rejection starves a person from love and acceptance that they were designed to receive. The problem is that when we turn to others or even ourselves for that love and acceptance, we are setting ourselves up for failure and the damage of rejection. Only God can be trusted as the source of our identity (L, 2003-2008).

Self-rejection is another piece to this puzzle. Self-rejection is where a person rejects them-self. They do not like who they are. This can often lead to self-hate, self-resentment, et cetera. It is often tied in with self-unforgiveness, if the person has made mistakes in their life that they deeply regret. Just as it hurts when others reject us, it can do just as much damage when we reject ourselves (L, 2003-2008).

Then there's perceived rejection, where a person receives something as rejection when it really isn't. For example, "Why is that person not coming over here to talk to me?" The person may not be trying to reject you, but may be shy at the time in stepping out and meeting you (or anybody else for that matter). People who have Spirits of Rejection can have a tendency to receive perceived rejection, because the purpose of a Spirit of Rejection is to make us feel rejected (L, 2003-2008).

A person who feels like God is always angry at them usually has issues of rejection. Perceived rejection can also make a person feel as if God has rejected him or her. This is a very common scene that we encounter in the deliverance ministry (L, 2003-2008).

Let's say that you are basing your identity on what your mother and father think of you. Now the moment that any hint of disapproval comes from them concerning you, it is going to hurt because they are the source of your identity. Anytime we base our identity on what we think of ourselves, or what others think of us, we virtually trust that person with our identity. We, ourselves, aren't capable of truly determining who we are; only God is qualified for that job. That is why it is absolutely vital for us to understand the person that God has made in us, and who we are as new creations in Christ Jesus. We were never made to live apart from God or base our identity on things of this world (L, 2003-2008).

When we base our identity upon what the Word of God has to say about us, we will become virtually rejection-proof. We can become immune from the wounds of rejection as long as we are not basing our identity upon what a person thinks of us (L, 2003-2008).

The closer a person is to you the deeper their rejection can wound you. Authority figures are also able to deeply wound you, because you look up to them and rely upon them. Parents often pass rejection on to their children when they say things such as, "I'll love you when you get good grades." Conditional love causes feelings of rejection and bondages such as performance orientation and drivenness (L, 2003-2008).

Whether you love or hate a person does not immune a person from rejection. You can literally want to kill somebody, but still be affected by their rejection. The question is: are you looking to them for approval? Are you basing your identity upon what they think of you? Does their approval of you give your life meaning and purpose (L, 2003-2008)?

A person's age also has a lot to do with their vulnerability to rejection. Children are especially vulnerable to the damage of rejection, because they are still developing their identity and learning about who they are. A lot of damage is done by peers in school. Either you're too short, too tall, too fat, and too skinny, you have brown eyes when you should have blue eyes...you name it, and kids will pick on it (L, 2003-2008)!

Insecure children can be very cruel and damage other children through rejection. Why? Because their own identity is not based on the right things. They do not know who they really are, or who they are called to be, so they go around putting other kids down to make themselves feel better. If they knew who they were in Christ, it would be an entirely different story! They would seek to edify other kids and help them find their identity and calling as well (L, 2003-2008).

Is it possible to receive rejection from a child or even a grandchild? Yes! Nobody is immune, providing that they are basing their identity on what that other person thinks of them. You can be 100 years old and be damaged by the rejection of a caretaker. Get your identity from God's Word (L, 2003-2008)!

As I mentioned earlier, it is vital that we base our identity, who we are, upon what God's Word says about us. When we do, we become virtually immune from the devastating and hurtful effects of rejection. God promises never to leave or forsake us, so when our identity is based upon what He says of us, we can be assured that we're not going to face rejection coming from Him (L, 2003-2008).

So what exactly does God's Word tell us about who we are in Christ?

- Because of God's great love for us, we are adopted into His family [1 John 3:1] and made joint heirs with Christ [Romans 8:17]

- We are made to sit in heavenly places (of authority over all demons, sickness, et cetera) with Christ [Ephesians 2:6]

- We are blessed with all spiritual blessings in Christ [Ephesians 1:3]

- We are the righteousness of Christ through faith, thus being made right before God [Romans 3:22]

- We are entitled to a clean conscience before God because of the Blood and we can have full assurance of faith when we go before Him [Hebrews 10:22]

- Our sins have been removed from us as far as the east is from the west [Psalms 103:12] and God Himself has chosen not to remember our failures [Hebrews 8:12]

- We are loved with the same love that the Father has for Jesus Himself! [John 17:23]

Can you identify with me in struggling with self-confidence? Low self-esteem? Purpose in life/church?

Dear Jesus,

_____

_____

_____

_____

_____

_____

_____

_____

_____

_____

_____

_____

_____

_____

_____

_____

_____

_____

_____

_____

_____

_____

_____

_____

_____

_____

_____

Sincerely,

    Me

Chapter 4

Picturing a Woman with a Painful Past: Where Do I Fit In?

Leah

A woman longing to be loved, looking for validation, yearning to be affirmed (Genesis 29:3-35). Validation, Affirmation, and Confirmation are gifts from the Lord. Leah struggled to feel fulfilled through her relationship with her husband and fell victim to the trap for validation through another. Six children; first three, this time he'll love me; fourth, now I will praise the Lord (Belt, et al., 2006).

We need to learn from Leah and avoid destructive actions and messages that bind, burden, and produce guilt and shame. We have internalized these disparaging messages and now find ourselves laboring in arenas that God never created us to labor in. To internalize violence is to become the victim and forgetting that every human life is a reflection of divinity. To internalize the abuse is to forget the divine testimony proclaimed about us: "It was very good" (Genesis 1:31). To internalize the shame carried is to forget that God cared enough to shape and make us in our mother's womb (Job 31:15; Psalm 22:9-10). Internalizing the violence causes self-blame and destroys the ability to see ourselves evolving. Internalizing negativity blocks us from realizing our tremendous creative potential that mirrors the divine impulse to beget life.

We have creative potential to bring forth life not only in procreation but also through our spirit and through our thoughts. We can let go of old destructive patterns that limit the Holy Spirit within us and curb intellectual, psychological, and emotional development. As reflections of God, we have the propensity to love, forgive, and show patience with ourselves and others (Belt, et al., 2006).

Hagar

Battered, Beaten, and Rejected but not abandoned. God provided for Hagar and her son, and he can and will provide for you (Belt, et al., 2006). One of the issues women face is the fear of abandonment. Each experience we construe as desertion can leave us doubting our self-worth. God cares and understands. He experienced the full scope of human despair and cannot help but be touched by our weaknesses (Hebrews 4:14-16). During God's time on earth, in the person of Jesus Christ, he too struggled with issues of abandonment. Jesus' own followers deserted him in his darkest hour (Matthew 26:55-56, 69-75) and He was betrayed to death by one of his own disciples (Matthew 26:14, 47-50).

During the times he needed His Father the most, at Gethsemane and Golgotha, Jesus cried out in the depths of mortal anguish, "My soul is overwhelmed with sorrow to the point of death...My Father, if it is possible, may this cup be taken from me"(Mt 26:38-39). The analogy of "this cup" signifies what all of us must go through in order to fulfill God's purpose in our lives. Whether "this cup" is childhood molestation, broken father-daughter relationships, death, loneliness, rejection, abandonment, divorce, et cetera, we must remember that it is up to us to see "this cup" as half empty or half full. In other words, do you see "this cup" as a stumbling block or stepping stone?

Just as Jesus arose from the dead in victory, we too can rise from the grip of despair and experience victory over our feelings of rejection (Belt, et al., 2006). We are not obsolete from the power of God to heal us. We do not have to be bound by the emotional chains of rejection. We can overcome and be victorious over our feelings of rejection just as Jesus did:

1. Relieve ourselves of guilt and any inappropriate sense of responsibility over circumstances that were to some extent beyond our control or not our fault.

2. Find comfort in God's love. Psalms 27:10, even when our parents forsake us, husband walks out, father who never showed up, mother who didn't care. We are wonderfully and fearfully made (Psalms 139:14).

3. Hebrews 13:5, He will never leave us or forsake us.

Dinah

An abused woman, breaking the silence of her rape; we have been abused in the name of love in so called loving relationships while those around us ignored our pain. Perhaps family members and friends are fully aware of the abuse but have chosen to turn away in silence (Genesis 34:7). They declared that the violation of one woman is an affront to the entire community; remove Dinah from the place of violation. We need to have the same anger that Dinah's brothers did when we hear of violence towards our abused sisters. We too can declare that physical and mental abuse is unacceptable and that it offends the entire community. We must not be silent (Belt, et al., 2006).

Sexual abuse is probably the most violent, brutal, and degrading form of suffering. Flashbacks and night terrors rob you of sleep. Sounds, sights, smells, and touches trigger old memories. You might be constantly blamed, shamed, and misunderstood. The emotional pain might become so intense that it causes you to consider ending your life or the life of your abusers. Yet, you are not alone, and God's word offers help (Belt, et al., 2006).

The Bible records acts of sexual abuse. Tamar was raped by her half-brother Amnon who at one time said he loved her (2 Samuel 13:1-22) and Dinah was raped by a Hivite prince, who also said he loved her (Genesis 34:1-4). Regardless of what these violent perpetrators said then and what modern-day perpetrators say today, violence and abuse do not equal love.

Healing from sexual abuse is not an easy process and it takes time and understanding to stop feeling like a victim. It might take years of crying, praying, journaling, yelling, screaming, and counseling to improve your self-esteem and emotional health. During that time, you must find a way to deal with your mind, body, and soul. You need to nurture yourself. During your time of healing you can find comfort and encouragement in knowing that God will never leave you nor forsake you (Deuteronomy 31:6; Isaiah 41:10).

Be assured that God is in control of your life. You can let go of the memories of abuse and you can become whole. Focus on living one day at a time before your loving God. God will send trustworthy people to journey with you and assist you in your healing. Love yourself. Trust yourself. Love and trust God. He is with you and will never leave you. God knows, cares, and understands (Belt, et al., 2006).

The scriptures do not offer any easy solutions to suffering. However, we should look at the way Christ handled suffering. He should be our model. The suffering he experienced on this earth and the heavenly victory he celebrates today shows us that our suffering is not in vain. With God's help, we also will have the victory (Belt, et al., 2006).

The Levite's Concubine

There are countless women around us today who are broken into many pieces. They have suffered horrors, violence, and abuse. Many of these women darken the doors of our churches and ministries; often they remain anonymous, unheard, and unspoken to. They literally are standing at the threshold crying out for help and we step over them and continue on our own journeys just as the Levite tried to do (Judges 19:27). If you feel broken and wonder if anyone even knows your name, remember that God knows who you are. When society continues to rob you of your dignity, God is able to take every broken piece of your life and bring about wholeness (Belt, et al., 2006).

Tamar

Someone betrayed our trust, someone manipulates our generosity, and before we know it we're left living with the consequences of other people's poor choices and sinful acts. Our brokenness can be restored and our tragedies can become testimonies of the true, unconditional love of Christ (2 Samuel 13:7-20; Mark 12:30-31). "Love the Lord your God with all your heart..." Love your neighbor as yourself. There is no commandment greater than these. Too often we overlook the requirement included in the second commandment. We must love ourselves. We are valuable to God and his sacrifice for you demonstrates that indisputable fact. No matter what you've been told, what you have experienced, or what mistakes you have made, God loves you and wants you to love yourself and be loved by others (Belt, et al., 2006).

Suffering covers a wide spectrum of circumstances. A woman's life is inextricably tied to suffering, making it impossible to live without the experience. Someone else's suffering may not be the same as yours, but you share a common bond through the mutual feelings suffering produces. Suffering may often be characterized as an experience of desolation; an emptiness, barrenness, aloneness. Suffering may take the form of an experience of separation from God, from other people, and even from engagement in living. Suffering is often an experience of desperation--a longing for life as we once knew it--often accompanied by the acknowledgement and understanding that life will in fact never be quite the same. Suffering even in its lesser degrees could be termed "life-threatening." It threatens our souls, our minds, and our hearts. The resulting disappointment and disillusionment can poison our thoughts and feelings, threatening our ability to live an abundant life (Belt, et al., 2006).

When we suffer we tend to become disheartened as we search for understanding. We question and cry out in despair only to discover a self we may not want to recognize; an angry, hateful, vengeful self but a true self nonetheless. In addition, we are likely to encounter a weak, humbled, needy, dependent, longing aspect of our-self. All the while in and through suffering we discover a self who understands, perhaps for the first time, that without God there is no life (Belt, et al., 2006).

Faith is the thread that maintains the balance between our life, as a whole, and our suffering. In our suffering faith becomes the hinge to the door of life, the vein that carries life to our soul. Our affliction comes as a test of our profession of faith in God through Jesus Christ. And with it comes a unique opportunity for us to glorify God (Belt, et al., 2006).

Do you have problems with letting go of past hurts? Are you bound by unforgiveness? Are you still living as the victim and not the victor?

Dear Jesus,

_____

_____

_____

_____

_____

_____

_____

_____

_____

_____

_____

_____

_____

_____

_____

_____

_____

_____

_____

_____

_____

_____

_____

_____

_____

_____

_____

Sincerely,

    Me

Chapter 5

Forgiveness: The Doorway to Healing and Reconciliation

One of life's greatest challenges is finding within ourselves the willingness to forgive someone who has hurt us. Offenses range from the uncomfortable to the unbearable. Sometimes the pain can be extreme. Yet when someone asks you for forgiveness, you may have an obligation as a Christian to grant it. Forgiveness of others' offenses against us is a prerequisite for God's forgiveness of our offenses against him (Matthew 6:14-15; James 2:13). God showed the world the ultimate act of forgiveness when he allowed his Son, Jesus Christ, to die for our sins. When love seems absent, because we are overwhelmed by negative feelings, we can remember that we are to forgive by faith, which is not necessarily accompanied by feelings. Even if we don't feel love for those who have wronged us, we can trust God to help us (Belt, et al., 2006).

We are called to remember that we in ourselves embody the gift of forgiveness. This gift flowed to us from God at Calvary! It was given to us as human beings before we even asked for it. Romans 5:10 says "when we were God's enemies, we were reconciled to him through the death of his Son." Just as God, in Christ, forgave us before we even knew to ask for forgiveness, so we are called to forgive others before we are asked. In many cases those who have wronged us will never ask for, or deserve, our forgiveness. However, if we wish for both, ourselves and our "debtors"(Matthew 6:12), to be healed from the hurt we will give the gift that not only makes individual healing possible but also allows for a possible reconciliation of relationships (Belt, et al., 2006).

Forgiveness is an act of faith. It is faith in a God that would allow abuse to happen, and faith that God would deal with the victimizer and heal the abused. Forgiveness brings freedom. Forgiveness means to release or set free.

Intellectually you can confront, sit the person down, write letters, but if you are not going through the pain and release of forgiveness, you are not free. Even if the person dies, you are not free. Forgiveness brings freedom to trust, freedom from fear and suspicion, freedom from bitterness, freedom from guilt and shame, freedom from embarrassment, freedom to tell the truth. Forgiveness is like turning the light on the secrecy of abuse (Stone, 2004).

Forgiveness is empowering. It is a powerful thing to be able to say, "I choose to forgive." You didn't have a choice in being victimized. Here you have a choice. Leave the vengeance to God. Oftentimes we want to determine how God deals with perpetrators. We want to set the sentence and the punishment. Some will deal with the court system, of course, but for so many others, the person that is guilty of violating you, will never pay for the sin or crime committed against you, simply because they will never have an understanding of the depth of your pain. Even if you blow their head off, you're not making them pay. Know that God handles this. That's where faith comes in (Stone, 2004).

To forgive is not easy, but it is possible. Be willing to let go of grudges and resentments over past hurts, to pray for the offender, to surrender the pain to God, and thus to serve as a channel for God's grace. Most important, forgiveness is the doorway to reconciliation. If we desire to live reconciled lives--at peace with God and creation--we will share this gift as often as necessary. A forgiving spirit blesses both, our self and others (Belt, et al., 2006).

According to Mary Parks (2006) there are several steps to healing and deliverance. As with any problem, the first step toward victory is to realize a problem exists. There is no record of Jesus casting out demons unless they were first recognized, either by the person being victimized, or by an authority over them (e.g. a parent).

The second step is to embrace the blood of Jesus. His blood is sufficient! Jesus won the victory for us when he hung on the cross, and "by His stripes we are healed" (Isaiah 53:5). There is no victory apart from the blood of Jesus (Parks, 2006).

The third step is remembering that Satan can only gain influence over us through the flesh, we must learn to lay down the "old man", the carnal nature – "die to self". Then, in submission to God, let Him bring forth the new creature we became when we accepted Jesus as savior and Lord, thereby we truly begin to "walking in the Spirit". Satan has no access when we are "possessed" by the Spirit of God. This may be the most important step and one not widely taught (Parks, 2006).

There is a difference between "patching up the old man" and "renewing the mind". Forgiveness, repentance, and spiritual warfare are required to bring forth the renewing of the mind. Forgiveness is just as important as warring against demonic forces because it destroys the "gate", or point of access, the enemy uses to gain a foothold (stronghold) in the victim's life. The past must be put behind to allow the Lord to heal. A deep emotional hurt, which can be a perceived one and not a factual one, is usually at the root of the problem. To forgive the hurt at the root of the problem takes the "axe to the root" (Luke 3:9). Forgive the person (ourselves included) involved and forgive God. This may sound strange, but anger toward God for what has happened to us, to hurt us, may be the actual root of the problem (Parks, 2006)!

Repentance is necessary for allowing Satan controlling access to the soul and for the hurt caused to ourselves and others. Though usually not a conscious decision more faith and trust has been put in the demonic stronghold than in God. The damage caused to ourselves and others by acting under the control of this spirit is a sin against man. The lack of trust and faith in God is a sin against God. Jesus said "You shall love the Lord your God above all else, and your neighbor as yourself" (Matthew 23:37-40). 1 John 1:9 says, "If we confess our sins, He is faithful and just to forgive us our sins and cleanse us of all unrighteousness." Repentance brings God's forgiveness, which brings cleansing and healing (Parks, 2006).

Warfare through intimacy with God, praise and worship, and direct confrontation of the enemy is also needed. The enemy is not going to give up his stronghold without a fight--he must be resisted. His influence must be renounced. James 4:8 says, "draw near to God, and He will draw near to you." And James 4:7 says, "submit yourselves therefore to God. Resist the devil, and he will flee from you." When submitted to God, we have authority over the devil (Parks, 2006).

> 2 Corinthians 10:3-5 *"For though we walk in the flesh, we do not war after the flesh: (For the weapons of our*

warfare are not carnal, but mighty
through God to the pulling down of
strong holds;) Casting down
imaginations, and every high thing
that exalteth itself against the
knowledge of God, and bringing into
captivity every thought to the
obedience of Christ."

When you draw near to God in intimate fellowship, the enemy must leave, for it is written "no evil dwells with Thee" (Psalm 5:4). Praise and worship releases God's power to do battle for you (2 Chronicles 20:20-30). This is especially critical when wrestling with principalities and powers (Parks, 2006).

Finally, in a step often overlooked in many teachings, the Holy Spirit must be sought to "renew the mind" completely in this area (Romans 12:2). Old habit patterns that were established while in bondage must be removed and replaced with a godly pattern. While the mind is being renewed, after deliverance, there is usually a period of "reconstruction". Recognize that this period must take place, and may require a lot of time. Yes, God can and does instantly deliver, but for us to stay in victory there is more often a progressive work - the transforming work of the Holy Spirit. This step "fills the void" left by the enemy, preventing a future attack worse than the original problem (Parks, 2006).

Are you harboring unforgiveness in your life? Are you willing to forgive without an apology? Is this unforgiveness keeping you from enjoying healthy relationships? It's time for you to release and exhale.

Dear Jesus,

_____

_____

_____

_____

_____

_____

_____

_____

_____

_____

Sincerely,

_Me_

Chapter 6

Recovering from Rejection

God understands rejection and knows how to remedy its pain. Christ was rejected when He came to His own people and they would not receive Him. *"He came to that which was his own, but his own did not receive him"* (John 1:11). He endured rejection when He bore our sins (Wood, 2008). *"He was despised and rejected by men, a man of sorrows, and familiar with suffering. Like one from whom men hide their faces he was despised, and we esteemed him not"* (Isaiah 53:3).

In other words, he specifically included in His suffering the substitutionary pain that was required to relieve us of our rejection. He bore it so we don't have to. On the cross, He felt the pain of being cut off from his heavenly Father; *"My God, my God, why hast thou forsaken me?"* (Matthew 27:46).

God understands your feelings. Therefore, He can be touched with your pain and is ready to heal you (Wood, 2008). *"For we do not have a high priest who is unable to sympathize with our weaknesses, but we have one who has been tempted in every way, just as we are-- yet was without sin. Let us then approach the throne of grace with confidence, so that we may receive mercy and find grace to help us in our time of need"* (Hebrews 4:15-16).

Diagnosing Rejection

According to Ron Wood (2008), here's how to diagnose if you suffer from the Spirit of Rejection. Three areas to examine are circumstances, emotions, and thoughts.

Let's start with your circumstances. Did you have an alcoholic parent? Were your parents divorced? Were you abused? Have you been abandoned or betrayed in marriage? Have you suffered from discrimination? Have you had to break away from a controlling relationship?

Have you been repeatedly de-valued as a person? If you fit any of these categories, then you could be a victim of the rejection syndrome (Wood, 2008).

Now let's consider your <u>emotional hot-buttons</u>. Do you have great difficulty receiving correction? Do you take it personal and get offended? Do you resent all authority? Do you get angry for no apparent reason? Or, do you have an unnatural need for everyone to like you? Does the need for approval control your decisions? Does insecurity sweep over you? Are you plagued by chronic self-doubt? Do you wrestle with chronic bouts of loneliness? At times, do you desire life, or are you tempted to take your own life? If so, then you probably battle rejection (Wood, 2008).

In addition to these diagnostic questions, ask your-self this about your <u>thought life</u>: *What kind of thoughts run through your mind when you are with a group of people?* Would you characterize these thoughts as mostly negative or positive? The Spirit of Rejection inserts these kinds of thoughts: "These people don't love me." "They won't talk to me." "I'm not worthy to be here." "I know they are judging me." "They don't really want me here." This is mental torment that typifies the spirit of rejection.

Inner Healing & Deliverance

If these questions point to your problem as the Spirit of Rejection, then you need to take it to God in prayer. If the problem persists, get someone to pray with you for deliverance. But first, realize this, rejection often carries with it unforgiveness toward those who have offended you. We might have been an innocent victim, but we have to take responsibility now for our reactions. We can't do away with our will and our choices or our reactions. We can be sinned against, begin to cherish a grudge, and as a result, begin to sin against our oppressors. *Unforgiveness in itself is a sin* (Wood, 2008).

God's grace will enable you to make a choice, to give forgiveness to all those for whom you hold grudges.

This is important! Freedom won't come without this vital step of forgiving others. In this case, your forgiveness must be explicit, by name, and it must be spoken aloud even if it is only to God, and even if it is for someone who is now dead. That does not matter. God is the judge of the living and the dead. Don't make any exceptions (Wood, 2008).

Don't allow any resentment to remain in your heart. Healing begins with a decision to repent and to give undeserved forgiveness. Give away grace and God will give grace to you. Repent of all bitterness and hatred (Wood, 2008).

When forgiveness is totally accomplished, it paves the way for successful inner healing. Inner healing is the actual curing of your soul of the wounds and traumas you have suffered and accumulated. The finger of God touches the sore spots and makes them well. This is the transformation of the inner man, the end to unrighteous reactions and automatic defenses. It is being at peace in Christ (Wood, 2008).

Inner healing must accompany deliverance. The place where damaged emotions have given way to this mind-set of rejection must be torn down, or else deliverance will be merely temporary. The house of your thought life must be swept and cleaned, then occupied with God's reassuring truth and love. Determine to think God's thoughts. This is a decision you must make in order to be free. Automatic judgments, racial prejudices, and defensive reactions need to be removed (Wood, 2008).

Take all negative thoughts captive. Don't let them rule over your mind. Replace them with words and images of faith that come from your heavenly Father. Take God's thoughts, God's attitude, God's will as your creed, not the words of this sinful world (Wood, 2008).

Repeat what the Scriptures say until they replace the lies you've heard. Soak in God's word and let it renew your mind. Meditate on the Scriptures until faith, hope, and self-acceptance fills your personality. This takes time but it is something you can do for yourself (Wood, 2008).

Renounce the Spirit of Rejection and stand against it. To renounce means to take a stand against something that you had previously been identified with or had claim to. Like renouncing your citizenship, it is a legal action that has power to affect your status. Pray aloud and say with your own words that rejection will not rule over you. Ask God for His fatherly affirmation. Ask God to give you the Spirit of Adoption. Every child needs to hear their father's voice saying, "You're mine and I love you" (Wood, 2008)!

After you've prayed against rejection, read the Scriptures, especially the epistles of the New Testament. They teach us our new identity in Christ, to "lay aside the old self" and "be renewed in the spirit of your mind" (Ephesians 4:22). Replace Satan's lies with God's word. Soak your thoughts in the truth of who God is, what He has done for you, and who you are in Christ. Banish all self-doubts. Tell yourself the truth until you truly believe it. Find new friends in Christ who affirm you and love you with God's love (Wood, 2008). *"See how great a love the Father has bestowed upon us, that we should be called the children of God"* I John 3:1.

The Spirit of Adoption

To understand the Spirit of Rejection we need to understand its opposite, which is the Spirit of Adoption. In the Bible, Romans chapter eight speaks of God's antidote to the Spirit of Rejection. This cure comes from our Heavenly Father, through the grace of our Lord Jesus, and is born witness to by the Holy Spirit. It is called the Spirit of Adoption. This is the Holy Spirit telling us that God the Father loves us and Jesus accepts us (Wood, 2008).

Sin and suffering cause people to be cut off from God and mistreat one another. Many unsaved adults are mad at God or are so deeply hurt that they blame God. This resentment keeps them from feeling God's love. Their image of God is wrong so they refuse to accept Him. God's grace offers us pardon even while we are angry and sinning. God knows we need to be healed of the consequences of our sins and the injuries of sins committed against us by others, even our parents. The Spirit of Adoption comes from heaven's throne. It can also be mediated by unconditional acceptance through other Christians. When we accept one another in Christ, relationships in Christ's body are formed. The Holy Spirit connects us together and affirms our self-worth. We are empowered to appreciate each other (Wood, 2008).

God's merciful provision for our healing comes by Christ's atonement on the cross. It is made real and effective in our lives when we confess our sins and receive His forgiveness. Then the Holy Spirit comes into our heart and testifies that we have become God's child. He does this by bearing witness in our spirit that we are adopted by God.

This is the Spirit of Adoption. The Spirit of Adoption goes beyond believing that God loves us; it is the actual *felt* love of God, so that we are enabled to *know* that God loves us. It ends loneliness, literally, forever (Wood, 2008)!

This marvelous work of affirming who we are in Christ is the work of the Holy Spirit; the Spirit of Truth. He only bears witness to what is true. He testifies in our spirit that we are truly loved by God. The Holy Spirit uses the Scriptures as well as the affirming voice of God to tell us the truth about ourselves. God's voice will cause us to know God's thoughts towards us. Those thoughts, always in agreement with the Scriptures, will reprove us for our sin and will affirm us as His children, but will never condemn us or drive us away. God will always tell us the truth in a merciful way. Our response is to believe what God says. Believing the truth about what Jesus did for us and believing the truth about who we are in Christ sets us free.

We need to believe both aspects of the truth about Jesus and about ourselves (Wood, 2008).

The truth is God loves us! His love toward us is tremendous. He wants us to really know Him and He wants to dwell in our hearts. God wants us to have fellowship with Him without condemnation. He accepts us into His family by virtue of Christ's work on the cross. He gives us a new identity as His sons and daughters (Wood, 2008).

Unlike some earthly fathers who failed us, our Heavenly Father will never abandon us. He will not cast away His children. God maintains a relationship with His offspring so that we need never fear being rejected by Him. His love is steadfast. It is covenant love (Wood, 2008).

In Conclusion, Jesus refused to walk in the Spirit of Rejection (Morris, 2010). In essence, Jesus said, "I refuse to be identified by who rejects me. I will only be identified by who accepts me -- My Father in heaven."

Many of us have been rejected:

- Rejected by an earthly father

    o BUT Accepted by our Heavenly Father through faith in Christ -- "Never will I leave you; never will I forsake you" (Hebrews 13:5; Deuteronomy 31:6)

- Rejected by an earthly mother

    o BUT "I will pray the Father, and he shall give you another Comforter, that he may abide with you forever" (John 14:16)

- Rejected by an earthly brother or sister

    o BUT "there is a friend who sticks closer than a brother" (Proverbs 18:24)

- Rejected by a spouse

    o BUT Christ loved you and gave himself up for you (Ephesians 5:25)

- Rejected by children

  - BUT you can say with Jesus "Here am I, and the children God has given me" (Hebrews 2:13; Isaiah 8:18)

- Rejected by friends

  - BUT Jesus said, "I no longer call you servants . . . Instead, I have called you friends" (John 15:15)

- Perhaps you have been rejected in other ways BUT Jesus said, "Surely I will be with you always, to the very end of the age" (Matthew 28:20)

CAST OFF THE SPIRIT OF REJECTION!

- Matthew 5:43-45

  - v. 44 -- Love your enemies and pray for those who persecute you

- Matthew 6:9-15

  - o v. 14 -- For if you forgive men when they sin against you, your heavenly Father will also forgive you

- Romans 12:14-21

  v. 21 -- Overcome evil with good

MAKE THIS CONFESSION!

- Through faith in Christ, I am not rejected by God!

- No matter who on earth has rejected me, my Father in heaven will not reject me!

- I am not a reject -- I AM PART OF THE ROYAL FAMILY OF GOD!

What steps have you taken to recover from the Spirit of Rejection? Do you recognize this Spirit operating in your life? Are you willing to accept the Spirit of Adoption and rebuke the Spirit of Rejection?

Dear Jesus,

_____

_____

_____

_____

_____

_____

_____

_____

_____

_____

_____

_____

_____

_____

_____

_____

_____

_____

_____

_____

_____

_____

_____

_____

_____

_____

Sincerely,

    Me

Epilogue

"CLING…CLING…CLING…CLING…CLING!"

That's the sound of an empty glass. I pray that after reading and journaling with me that "your cup" is one step closer to being emptied; emptied from all of the hurt, guilt, shame, disappointment, regret, resentment, unforgiveness, depression, and bitterness that was spilling over into your relationships, jobs, and churches.

No matter of the unpleasant events that you have encountered or faced in life, you do not have to become a "victim" to it/them. Unhealthy relationships and feelings of inadequacy are tactics that the enemy tries to use to keep us from stepping into our destiny. If the devil can keep us focused on being victimized, unappreciated, and mistreated he knows that we will **never move past** our fleshly desires for belonging or feeling needed/wanted.

Masking our needs for approval and acceptance is prevalent in the church and it has been traditionally misdiagnosed or undiagnosed, until now. The fear of being rejected has kept us from confessing our unresolved issues and showing our "withered hand" (Matthew 12:9-14). Not dealing with the fact that I've been molested or that I've suffered from poor self-esteem, due to my broken relationship with my dad, was due to the controlling Spirit of Rejection. I was so consumed with "what was wrong with me" that I never acknowledged that anything was "right with me."

Do not let this happen to you. Begin your personal journey of healing and discover **"the why"** behind your hurt, pain, struggles, disappointment, anger, bitterness, shame, and guilt. The enemy has been hard at work trying to keep you from reaching your full potential in ministry. The enemy's whole mission is to keep you on a "detour!" When we bottle things up instead of discovering healthy ways to express your frustrations, temptations, and idealizations or imaginations we are yielding authority over to the enemy.

God revealed to me that instead of complaining, I needed to be thankful for the people that were right here around me. Despite what the research said, I married a faithful, loving, unselfish, supporting husband who cherishes me. I have 3 beautiful children who adore me, a mother who loves me unconditionally, and a sister who looks up to me. Seize your God-given power and authority and vow to never let **"YOUR CUP RUN OVER!"**

Bibliography

Belt, C., Thompson, J., Lee, L., Bryant, N., Coleman, M., Ward, C., et al. (2006). *NIV Aspire: The New Women of Color Study Bible*. Grand Rapids: Zondervan.

Freud, S. (1988). *My three mothers and other passions*. New York: New York University Press.

Kelly, J. (2003). *Dads and Daughters*. New York: Broadway.

L, R. (2003-2008). *How to Overcome rejection: Correcting Mistaken Identity*. Retrieved September 30, 2010, from Great Bible Study: http://www.greatbiblestudy.com/rejection.php

Langeland, R. (2004). *Healing the Wounded Heart*. Retrieved September 22, 2010, from Hidden with Christ Ministries: http://www.hiddenwithchrist.com/written/index.htm

Moody, G. a. (n.d.). *Rejection*. Retrieved September 30, 2010, from Demonbusters: http://www.moodymanual.demonbuster.com/reject.html

Morris, P. C. (2010, February 10). *The Spirit of Rejection*. Retrieved September 30, 2010, from Parkway Church of God: http://www.theparkwaychurch.org/blog/files/271523eede13d553be429696d4141946-1.html

Neilson, L. (2006). Fathers and Daughters: A Needed Course in Family Studies. *Marriage and Family Review Journal* , 1-11.

Parks, M. (2006, November 22). *Overcoming Rejection.* Retrieved September 30, 2010, from Breath Life: http://maryannparks.wordpress.com/2006/11/22/overcoming-rejection/

Perkins, R. M. (2001, December 1). *The father-daughter: familial interactions that impact a daughter's life-style.* Retrieved January 21, 2008, from Encyclopedia.com: http://www.encyclopedia.com/doc/1G1-84017198.html

Perry, T. (2009, October 8). *L.A. Rag Mag- We're on the Rag all the Time.* Retrieved November 4, 2009, from Tyler Perry, Queen Latifah, and Monique were Molested: http://laragmag.com/tyler-perry-queen-latifah-monique-were-molested.html

Secunda, V. (1992). *Women and their Fathers.* New York: Bantam Doubleday Dell.

Stone, R. (2004). *No Secrets No Lies, How Black Families Can Heal from Sexual Abuse.* New York: Broadway Books.

Wood, R. (2008, July 15). *Beating the Spirit of Rejection: The Spirit of Rejection.* Retrieved September 22, 2010, from My Space: http://blogs.myspace.com/index.cfm?fuseaction=blog.view&friendId=3004374&blogId=415122588

Additional Copies Can Be Purchased at:

www.drtandriacallins.com

www.heartinkpress.com

Other Published Works

Callins, T. & Shealey, M. (2007). "Creating Culturally Responsive Literacy Programs in Inclusive Classrooms". *Intervention in Schools and Clinic.* v42 n4 p195-197.

Callins, T. (2004). "Culturally Responsive Literacy Instruction". *National Center for Culturally Responsive Educational Systems* (NCCRESt) www.nccrest.org.

Callins, T. (2003). "Narrowing the Achievement Gap Through Family Literacy" *Southern Association of Equal Opportunity of Program Personnel* (SAEOPP). *XX*(8), 19-27.

Mays, W., McDonald, S., Briscoe, R., & Callins, T., (2003). "The Village Legacy". Community Resource Manual. Project Sponsored by the Children's Board of Hillsborough County THINK Grant and the Department of Child and Family Studies, U.S.F.